Conducting the Oracle Job Interview
IT Manager's Guide for Oracle Job Interviews with Oracle
Interview Questions

Mike Ault
Donald K. Burleson

We dedicate this book to our loving wives, Susan Ault and Janet Burleson, whose love and support made this book possible.

--- Mike Ault

--- Don Burleson

Conducting the Oracle Job Interview
IT Manager's Guide for Oracle Job Interviews with Oracle Interview Questions

By Mike Ault & Donald K. Burleson

Copyright © 2003 by Rampant TechPress. All rights reserved.

Printed in the United States of America.

Published by Rampant TechPress, Kittrell, North Carolina, USA

Oracle In-Focus Series: Book #2

Series Editor: Don Burleson

Editors: Robert Strickland, John Lavender, and Linda Webb

Production Editor: Teri Wade

Cover Design: Bryan Hoff

Printing History:

February 2003 for First Edition

Oracle, Oracle7, Oracle8, Oracle8i, and Oracle9i are trademarks of Oracle Corporation. *Oracle In-Focus* is a registered Trademark of Rampant TechPress.

Many of the designations used by computer vendors to distinguish their products are claimed as Trademarks. All names known to Rampant TechPress to be trademark names appear in this text as initial caps.

ISBN: 0-9727513-1-9

Library of Congress Control Number: 2003090841

Table of Contents

Using the Online Code Depot

Your purchase of this book provides you with complete access to the online code depot that contains the sample tests and answers.

All of the job questions in this book are located at the following URL:

rampant.cc/job.htm

All of the sample tests in this book will be available for download in a zip format, ready to load and use on your database.

If you need technical assistance in downloading or accessing the scripts, please contact Rampant TechPress at info@rampant.cc.

Conventions Used in this Book

It is critical for any technical publication to follow rigorous standards and employ consistent punctuation conventions to make the text easy to read.

However, this is not an easy task. Within Oracle there are many types of notation that can confuse a reader. Some Oracle utilities such as STATSPACK and TKPROF are always spelled in CAPITAL letters, while Oracle parameters and procedures have varying naming conventions in the Oracle documentation. It is also important to remember that many Oracle commands are case sensitive, and are always left in their original executable form, and never altered with italics or capitalization.

Hence, all Rampant TechPress books follow these conventions:

- **Parameters** - All Oracle parameters will be *lowercase italics*. Exceptions to this rule are parameter arguments that are commonly capitalized (KEEP pool, TKPROF), these will be left in ALL CAPS.

- **Variables** – All PL/SQL program variables and arguments will also remain in lowercase italics (*dbms_job, dbms_utility*).

- **Tables & dictionary objects** – All data dictionary objects are referenced in lowercase italics (*dba_indexes, v$sql*). This includes all v$ and x$ views

(*x$kcbcbh,*   *v$parameter*)   and   dictionary   views
(*dba_tables,*   *user_indexes*).

- **SQL** – All SQL is formatted for easy use in the code depot, and all SQL is displayed in lowercase. The main SQL terms (select, from, where, group by, order by, having) will always appear on a separate line.

- **Programs & Products** – All products and programs that are known to the author are capitalized according to the vendor specifications (IBM, DBXray, etc). All names known by Rampant TechPress to be trademark names appear in this text as initial caps. References to UNIX are always made in uppercase.

Acknowledgements

This type of highly technical reference book requires the dedicated efforts of many people. Even though we are the authors, our work ends when we deliver the content. After each chapter is delivered, several Oracle DBAs carefully review and correct the technical content. After the technical review, experienced copy editors polish the grammar and syntax. The finished work is then reviewed as page proofs and turned over to the production manager, who arranges the creation of the online code depot and manages the cover art, printing distribution, and warehousing.

In short, the authors played a small role in the development of this book, and we need to thank and acknowledge everyone who helped bring this book to fruition:

- **John Lavender**, for the production management, including the coordination of the cover art, page proofing, printing, and distribution.

- **Robert Strickland**, for his excellent copyediting and format checking services.

- **Teri Wade**, for her help in the production of the page proofs.

- **Bryan Hoff**, for his exceptional cover design and graphics.

- **Janet Burleson,** for her assistance with the web site, and for creating the code depot and the online shopping cart for this book.

- **Linda Webb**, for her expert page-proofing services.

With our sincerest thanks,

Mike Ault & Don Burleson

Preface

After interviewing hundreds of candidates for Oracle-related positions, we are aware that it is getting harder to locate and retain qualified Oracle professionals. You must cull the best fit for the Oracle job from hundreds of resumes. Success depends upon knowing exactly which skills you need, and verifying that each candidate possesses acceptable levels of those skills.

That's where this book can help you. For both the new Oracle IT manager and the seasoned VP, the levels within the Oracle professional position will be explained to illustrate screening and interview techniques. Some common misconceptions will be clarified about the Oracle professional position and tips will be provided on how to interview a candidate for an Oracle professional position.

Large numbers of Oracle neophytes are obtaining Oracle DBA certification through the Oracle Certified Professional (OCP) program. This glut of OCP-certified Oracle professionals makes it more important than ever to evaluate every Oracle professional job candidate's experience and working knowledge of Oracle.

To help find, hire, and retain suitable Oracle professionals, background evaluation tips will be provided for identifying the best candidates. For the technical interview, sample technical questions and answers are also provided.

Of course, there is no magic formula for determining if a candidate can perform properly, and no single screening test to ensure that you will properly evaluate a candidate's ability. However, if the employer and candidate are properly prepared, then filling the position successfully becomes much less chancy.

It is our hope that this book will provide you with an indispensable tool for identifying, interviewing, and hiring top-notch Oracle professionals.

Chapter 1

Introduction to Oracle Professional Evaluation

As Oracle began to dominate the database market, hundreds of thousands of companies, from mom-and-pop grocery stores to multi-billion dollar corporations, began to embrace Oracle technology. This mushrooming need for Oracle professionals has created a vastly disparate job pool. Job skills range from Oracle DBAs with PhDs in Information Systems from top U.S. universities and 20 years' experience, to semi-literate Oracle trainees with 90 days' experience.

The result of the explosive growth of the Oracle industry is a two-tiered job market. Many top-rated universities teach Oracle as part of their undergraduate CS or IT curriculum and produce Oracle professionals for career tracks in large corporations.   At the same time, trade schools and community colleges produce hundreds of thousands of Oracle programmers and developers. No matter what the economic climate, large corporations actively recruit their entry-level talent for their mission-critical Oracle roles from prestigious universities.

Preparing the Oracle Job Offering

One of the points that we repeatedly make is that top-notch Oracle professionals are hard to find and well compensated, while mediocre Oracle professionals are easy to find and hire.

On the high end, Oracle DBAs with over 10 years' experience and graduate degrees typically command salaries ranging from $75,000 to $140,000 per year, depending on geographical location. For Oracle DBA consultants with a broad exposure in mission-critical areas, the sky is the limit. For example, Oracle Corporation charges $475/hour for experienced on-site Oracle consultants, and self-made Oracle millionaires are not uncommon.

On the other end of the spectrum, we see overseas Oracle trainees who will work remotely from Bangalore, India for as little as $10/per hour, and OCP certified beginners who are desperate for a chance to learn Oracle on your multi-million dollar production database.

The first step in hiring an Oracle professional is determining the level of skill you require and preparing an incentive package. If your database is mission-critical, then a seasoned Oracle professional is your safest choice, and people with high skill levels often require incentives to abandon their employers.

Preparing the Incentive Package

If you want a top-notch senior Oracle professional, you may be surprised to find them in short supply, even in a tight job market. While every manager knows that salary alone cannot guarantee employee loyalty, there are a host of techniques used by IT management to attract and retain the top-notch Oracle professional.

In addition to a competitive salary, some of the techniques used to entice potential Oracle professionals include:

- **Flex time** - Burnout can be a real problem among the Oracle professionals who must typically work evenings and holidays to maintain the computer systems. Many companies offer formal comp-time policies or institute a four-day workweek, allowing the Oracle professional to work four, 10-hour days per week.

- **Telecommuting** - Many Oracle professionals are allowed to work at home and only visit the office once per week for important face-to-face meetings.

- **Golden handcuffs** - Because a high base salary does not always reduce attrition, many Oracle managers use yearly bonuses to retain employees. Golden handcuffs may take the form of a Management by Objective (MBO) structure, whereby the Oracle professional receives a substantial annual bonus for meeting management expectations. Some companies implement golden handcuffs by paying the employee a huge signing bonus (often up to $50,000) and requiring the employee to return the bonus if he or she leaves the company in less than three years. However, don't be surprised to find that some competing companies will reimburse the Oracle professional to repay a retention bonus.

- **Office perks** - Since many senior Oracle professionals command salaries commensurate with those received by corporate vice presidents, some senior Oracle DBAs are offered private offices and company cars.

- **Fancy job titles** - Because Oracle professionals command high salaries, many are given honorary job titles. These include "fellows" titles such as the Apple fellow, whereby the corporation grants special privileges to Oracle employees who have been granted fellow status. Other Oracle professional titles include vice president of database administration, chief technologist, and the new job title (used by Bill Gates), chief software architect.

- **Specialized training** - Oracle professionals are commonly rewarded by sending them to conferences and training classes, and an entire industry is built around these large Oracle events. For example, Oracle Applications conferences are held in Hawaii, and Oracle cruises have become an extremely popular reward for the Oracle professional. The Geek Cruise Line is typical of this movement, offering technical conferences on hot topics in Oracle, Java, and Perl, combined with an ocean cruise. Companies pack these cruise ships with their Oracle professionals, sailing to exotic destinations in Alaska, Hawaii, and the Mediterranean.

Defining the Required Job Skills

A number of Oracle professionals mistakenly believe that the Oracle DBA job is purely technical. In reality, the Oracle DBA must be an "ace" of all IT functions, because he or she has ultimate responsibility for overall database design, database implementation, backup, and recovery. Excellent communications, as well as technical skills, are required for the DBA's close involvement in all phases of project development.

Remember, knowledge of Oracle database systems is not enough. An understanding of operating systems and computer-science theory is imperative as well. That is why employers like to hire Oracle DBAs who also have a background in computer science, information systems, or business administration.

It's critical to remember that Oracle certification tells employers only that the job candidate successfully passed a certification test on the technical aspects of Oracle database administration. In the real world, Oracle certification is just one of many criteria used to evaluate an Oracle job candidate. Other criteria include the following:

- **Excellent Communication Skills** - The Oracle professional is the central technical guru for the Oracle shop. He or she must be able to explain Oracle concepts clearly to all developers and programmers accessing the Oracle database. In many shops, the Oracle DBA is also a manager and is required to have excellent communication skills for participating in strategic planning and database architectural reviews.

- **Formal Education** – Many employers require Oracle professionals to have a bachelor's degree in computer science or information systems. For advanced positions such as an Oracle DBA, many employers prefer a master's degree in computer science or a master's in business administration (MBA).

- **Real-World Experience** - This requirement is the catch-22 for newbies who possess only an OCP certificate. A common complaint of people who have OCP certificates but no job experience is that they cannot get experience without the OCP, and they cannot get a job without experience. This is especially true in a tight job market.

- **Knowledge of Database Theory** - In addition to mastering the technical details required for the OCP exams, the successful Oracle professional must have an understanding of database and data warehouse design. This includes intimate knowledge of data normalization theory and knowledge of star schema design, as well as object-oriented modeling with Unified Modeling Language (UML) and knowledge of other database design methodologies such as CORBA and J2EE.

The Code Depot Key is	raffles

Basic IT Skills

Because the Oracle professional is often called-upon to perform critical projects in the IT department, a broad background is often desirable. Much of this basic IT knowledge is taught in academic Computer Science and Information Technology programs. Non-Oracle job skills include:

- **System Analysis & Design** – Many Oracle professionals must take an active role in the analysis and design of new database systems. Hence, knowledge of data flow diagrams, data dictionary techniques, CASE tools, Entity-relation modeling and design techniques enhance the Oracle professional's scope of ability.

- **Database Design** – Many Oracle jobs require knowledge of database normalization theory, STAR schema design, and data modeling techniques.

- **Physical Disk Storage** – Understanding of disk hardware architecture, RAID implementation, cache controllers, and disk load balancing are beneficial to any Oracle professional.

- **Data Security Principles** – An understanding of relational database security, including role-based security, is useful, especially for US Government positions.

- **Backup and Recovery Techniques** – Many backup and recovery methods involve third-party software (Veritas, Legato, ADSM), and the candidate should have real-world experience implementing backup and recovery methods.

- **Change Control Management** – In many cases the Oracle professional is charged with the task of implementing change control and insuring that changes to the production database are properly coordinated. Knowledge of third-party change control tools, such as the UNIX Source Code Control System (SCCS), is beneficial.

Now that we understand the basic skills, let's talk about Oracle certification. The Oracle Certified Professional (OCP) exams identify candidates who have mastered specific technical areas within Oracle administration. However, as interviewers frequently discover, possession of the OCP is no guarantee that a candidate has real Oracle expertise.

Oracle Certified Professionals

Lured by the promise of big bucks, thousands of ordinary blue-collar people have managed to complete "Oracle boot camps" that teach them how to pass the OCP exams. From shoe salesmen to auto mechanics, people are getting certified by Oracle Corporation without the appropriate IT background. In one case, a newly minted OCP "fudged" their résumé and obtained a corporate Oracle position. This person seriously misunderstood the basic concepts of Oracle database administration and quickly caused a multi-million dollar production outage. Worst of all, the manager had to bring in extra consulting talent to set things straight and had to explain to HR why he was terminating an employee they had just paid $30,000 to relocate from another city. So then, what is the value of an OCP?

The Value of Oracle Certification

Starting with the obvious question, what is the value of Oracle certification? Considering that Oracle exams cost $125 each and that some certifications require up to five exams, and factoring in the cost of books, classes, and other study materials, Oracle certification is a sizable investment. However, the potential rewards can make that investment worthwhile.

Here's the catch - Oracle certification alone is not a guarantee that anyone will find employment in Oracle database administration. The Oracle certification is just one of the credentials valued by prospective employers.

The OCP DBA certifications are the most popular of all Oracle certifications. Originally, the Oracle7 certification exams were designed for working professionals. Candidates were required to supply written proof of DBA work experience for at least four years. However, Oracle has expanded the program, due to the explosive demand for Oracle professionals.

In Oracle9i, three levels of certification are offered by Oracle:

- **Oracle9i Certified Professional (OCP)** - The Oracle certified professional is required to pass four challenging exams and demonstrate proficiency in all technical areas of Oracle database administration.

- **Oracle Certified Associate (OCA)** - This lower-level certification is offered by Oracle for those candidates who successfully passed only two of the four OCP exams.

- **Oracle Certified Master (OCM)** - The candidate is required to attend Oracle training at *Oracle* University for this certification. This program is an offshoot of the former Oracle Masters program of the 1990s.

The OCM requires candidates to complete the following tasks:

- Earn an OCP certificate
- Take two advanced-level Oracle University classes
- Pass a pre-admission exam
- Pass a practicum exam in an Oracle lab environment

Training for Certification

The Oracle8i certification track requires a series of several exams, which cover the topics of SQL, PL/SQL, database administration, Oracle networking, backup and recovery, and Oracle performance tuning.

The Oracle certification program has evolved into a complex array of exams and certifications, and the exams continue to evolve with new Oracle releases. Both Oracle professionals and hiring managers can use the certifications as a gauge of competence, but real-world experience must never be discounted.

The OCP has come under criticism lately because Oracle allows one of the exams to be taken over the Internet without proctoring. Oracle also requires that at least one training class be taken at a school approved by Oracle University.

While the OCP is not a complete measure of a person's skills, it does demonstrate a modicum of talent and provides a method for those with degrees in Computer Science of Business Administration to enter the Oracle job field.

For an Oracle professional candidate, depth of knowledge in computer programming concepts is far more important than ability to pass the OCP exam. Employers are recognizing the pitfalls of hiring people based solely upon Oracle OCP certification.

Oracle Professional Characteristics

While many Oracle shops have hundreds of technology workers, retention efforts are normally focused on technical DBAs, whose knowledge of the company's systems is not easily transferred to replacements.

In many shops, Oracle DBAs typically serve many roles. In addition to traditional DBA duties, the Oracle DBA is often called upon to serve as a system architect, an Informaticist (a functional IT professional who possesses an MS in computer science and is also trained in professional areas, such as medicine or accounting), a database administrator, or a system administrator. In today's market, Medical Informaticists (an Oracle DBA with an MD degree) are the highest-paid and most sought-after of the Oracle DBAs, commonly earning over $200,000 per year.

The following attributes are signs of a top-notch Oracle professional:

- **Has earned at least one professional degree or certification** - Possessing a degree such as MD, JD, MBA, MSEE, or CPA, in addition to an Oracle degree, makes an employee a valuable asset, one difficult to replace in the open job market.

- **Has graduated from a competitive university** - Oracle professionals must be self-starting and highly motivated to be effective, and this is often indicated by entrance to competitive universities with rigorous admission standards. These schools include most Ivy League schools, especially MIT, and universities with stellar reputations in Information Systems such as Purdue, the University of Texas, the University of California at Los Angeles, the University of San Diego, and the University of California at Berkeley.

- **Is trained in a special skill** - Oracle professionals with specialized, difficult-to-find training are often in high demand. Examples of specialized skills are SAP, Oracle Applications, Java, Oracle9iAS, and J2EE.

- **Active in the Oracle community** - Many good Oracle professionals participate in local user groups, present techniques, and publish in many of the Oracle-related periodicals.

- **Is recognized as an Oracle expert** - A sure sign of an Oracle all-star is someone who gets in front of audiences by publishing a book, writing a magazine article, or appearing as a conference speaker.

- **Possesses irreplaceable knowledge of an institution's enterprise systems** - If the employee serves in a mission-critical Oracle role, such as chief architect or DBA, a vacuum in the Oracle department may be created by that employee's departure.

Sample Job Sheet for an Oracle DBA

Applicants for any Oracle job are expected to meet all of the requirements in mission-critical areas, including education, experience, certification, writing credits, personal characteristics, and legal standing. Here is an example Oracle job requirement sheet from an actual corporation:

Sample Oracle Job Sheet

These are the minimum job requirements for the position of Senior Oracle Architect. The HR department will pre-screen all candidates for the following job skills and experience.

Education

Persons with Masters Degrees, Doctoral degrees and Ivy League graduates are desired. At a minimum, the candidate is expected to possess a four-year degree from a fully-accredited university in a discipline such as Computer Science, Software Engineering, BA or MBA in Information Systems (from an AACSB accredited university), or Engineering (electrical, mechanical, or chemical).

Work Experience

The Oracle candidate is required to have a minimum of ten years of full-time, progressive experience in relational database administration and management.

OCP Certification

The Oracle candidate must have earned an Oracle certification at some time in the last ten years.

Publishing and Research

The candidate should show demonstrable interest in publishing Oracle research as evidenced by participating in user groups and publishing of articles, books and columns. These include:

Books. Oracle technical books or any other recognized academic publication company.

> *Articles for academic journals.* For example, the *Journal of the IEEE* and the *Journal of Information Systems.*

> *Conference papers.* Writing papers and presenting at conferences such as OracleWorld and Database World.

> *Articles in trade publications.* Writing an article for a trade Publication such as Oracle Magazine, Oracle

Internals, DM-Review, or Dr. Dobbs Journal.

Personal Integrity

This position requires securing mission-critical applications and accessing confidential data, and all candidates are required to sign a waiver to disclose personal information.

The Oracle candidate must have no history of acts of moral turpitude, drug use, dishonesty, lying, cheating, or theft.

USA Citizenship

We are unable to sponsor H1-B foreign consultants. Therefore, candidates must provide proof of US citizenship.

Additional Specialized Skills

The following specialized skills are desired:

- Masters or Doctorate degree from a major university
- An active US Secret, Top secret or Q-level security clearance
- Oracle Parallel Server (Oracle9i Real Application Clusters)
- SAP, Oracle Applications, or PeopleSoft Oracle DBA
- UNIX System Administration HP/UX, Solaris or AIX

As we can see, Oracle positions have requirements that vary widely, and it is up to the IT manager to choose those qualities that best suit the position.

Conclusion

This chapter has been concerned with identifying the job requirements and preparing an incentive list. Next, let's take a look at how to evaluate the Oracle professional for specific job skills.

Chapter 2

Qualities of the Successful Oracle Professional

The evaluation of the résumé is a critical part of the selection process. In a tight job market, it is not uncommon to receive hundreds of résumés, and it is the job of the HR or IT manager to fairly and efficiently pre-screen applicants and only forward qualified individuals to the IT manager for a detailed interview. Let's start by looking at techniques for evaluating the job history of an Oracle professional.

Evaluating Employment History

Evaluation of an Oracle job candidate's work history is the single most critical factor in résumé screening. Candidates without a significant work history may spend an undue amount of time learning their jobs, while a more expensive, experienced candidate may be a better overall value for the hiring company.

Not all Oracle experience is equal. Many demanding Oracle shops provide excellent training and experience, while others provide only glancing exposure to Oracle software.

When evaluating Oracle work experience, the following factors need to be considered:

- **Oracle job role** - Oracle candidates who have had positions of responsibility within their organization are often more qualified than those candidates for whom the Oracle skills were a part-time duty.

- **Employer-sponsored Oracle education** - Many large corporations require yearly training for all IT employees, and on-the-job education is a clear indicator of the employer's quality. Employer-sponsored, yearly Oracle training and participation in Oracle groups and conferences (IOUG, OracleWorld) are indications of a good background for an Oracle DBA.

Fraudulent Work History

In the soft market of the early twenty-first century, it is not uncommon for a desperate Oracle job applicant to forge a work history with a defunct dot-com. The desperate applicant hopes that this fraud will not be detected. This phenomenon presents the IT manager with a unique challenge in verifying employment history with a company that no longer exists or contacting job references who cannot speak English.

In many cases, the HR staff strongly discounts résumés where the employment and educational history cannot be completely verified. Many departments, frustrated with confirming overseas employment histories, never forward these types of résumés to the IT manager.

Evaluating Personal Integrity

It is always a good idea to perform a background check, which is easily obtained via national services. Many companies require that a candidate not have any criminal convictions, except minor traffic violations. In some cases, a routine background check can reveal arrests and acts of moral turpitude.

An Oracle professional's ongoing responsibilities often include securing mission-critical applications and confidential data. Therefore, some companies require that all applicants for Oracle professional positions be expected to demonstrate the highest degree of personal and moral integrity.

In addition, acts of moral turpitude, such as a history of drug use, dishonesty, lying, cheating, or theft may be grounds for immediate rejection. In some companies, all applicants are expected to sign a waiver to disclose personal information and are asked to submit to a polygraph exam.

Evaluating Academic History

While formal education is not always a predictor of success at an Oracle job, there can be no doubt that job candidates with advanced degrees from respected universities possess both the high intelligence and persistence needed in a top-notch Oracle professional.

Many IT shops save time by letting universities pre-screen Oracle professional candidates. For example, MIT carefully screens grades and achievement, and this pre-screening by the university allows companies to choose computer science professionals with increased confidence in a candidate's required skills.

The type of Oracle job to be filled may determine the academic history required. For example, an Oracle developer/programmer may not require a four-year degree, while a lead Oracle DBA for a large corporation may need a Master's degree from a respected university.

Note: This section is based upon the author's experience in evaluating Oracle professionals and the HR policies of large Oracle shops. This section is in no way meant to discredit those Oracle job applicants without the benefit of a college education.

Rating College Education

Many shops have an HR professional evaluate education, while other IT managers take it upon themselves to evaluate the quality of the Oracle candidate's formal education. Fortunately, sources for rating colleges and universities can be found online. Many large corporations require that the job candidate's degree must be from a university possessing a first-tier or second-tier rating by US News & World Report's "America's Best Colleges" or degrees from exceptional universities (as listed in the Gourman Report).

Of course, not all Oracle jobs require a college degree. For lower-level Oracle jobs, the formal academic requirements are less challenging, but the lead DBA for a large corporation must possess high intelligence, superb communications skills, and the drive and persistence that is most commonly associated with someone who has taken the time to invest in a quality education.

College Major and Oracle Job Suitability

There is a great deal of debate about what academic majors, if any, are the best indicators of success in an Oracle professional position. However, it is well documented that different majors attract students with varying abilities. The following list describes some indicators used in large corporations for assessing the relative value of different college majors:

- **Engineers**. Engineers tend to make great Oracle professionals, especially those with degrees in Electrical Engineering (EE). An engineering curriculum teaches logical thinking and data structure theory that makes it easy for the engineer to learn Oracle quickly. However, while engineers have unimpeachable technical skills, their oral and written communication skills are often lacking. Therefore, IT managers should pay careful attention to communication skills when interviewing Oracle applicants with engineering degrees.

- **Business Majors**. Business majors make excellent Oracle developers and analysts because of their training in finance, accounting, marketing, and other business processes. Many business schools also require matriculated students to take several courses in Information Technology. Not all college business schools are equal, though. When screening an Oracle job applicant with a business major, time should be taken to insure that the degree is from a business school accredited by the American Assembly of Collegiate Business Schools (AACSB). There are many fly-by-night business schools, and their depth of training may be vastly different.

- **Computer Science Majors.** Computer scientists typically receive four years of extensive technical training, and are ideal candidates for Oracle jobs requiring in-depth technical ability. However, like the engineers, many computer scientists have sub-standard communications skills.

- **Music Majors.** For many years, IBM recruited from the ranks of college musicians because hiring managers found that musicians possessed an ability in logical thinking that made them ideal candidates for IT skill training.

- **Math Majors.** Math majors tend to possess excellent logical thinking skills and often possess a background in computer science. Like many quantitative majors, social and communications skills may be a concern.

- **Education Majors.** Evaluation of education majors is extremely difficult because of the wide variation in quality between universities. Nationally, GRE test rankings by academic major show that education majors consistently rank in the lowest 25% of knowledge. Any applicant with an education major should be carefully screened for technical skills, and the college ranking checked in US News & World Report's "America's Best Colleges".

International Degrees

A huge variation in quality exists among international degrees. Therefore, Oracle professional candidates with international degrees should be carefully checked in the "Gourman Report" of International Colleges and Universities.

Some sub-standard overseas colleges have no entrance requirements and require little effort from the student. There has also been a rash of résumé falsifications of college degrees from overseas colleges. The fraudulent applicant is often relying upon the human resource department's inability to successfully contact the overseas school to verify the applicant's degree.

In sum, international degrees should be carefully evaluated. It is recommended that, where appropriate, foreign language professionals be hired to write the letters to request verification of the graduate's attendance, and to obtain and translate the college transcript.

Advanced Degrees and Oracle Professionals

Approximately 30% of Oracle DBAs for large corporations possess an advanced degree (Masters or Doctorate). While an advanced degree shows dedication to a professional position, the quality of the degree is of paramount concern.

A higher ranking should be given to an on-site master's degree from a respected university than to a night school or "non-traditional" graduate school. These non-traditional schools often have far lower acceptance standards for students and are far less academically demanding than the top US graduate programs.

Personality of the Oracle DBA

What is more important to managers, technical knowledge or personality? Many times, managers concentrate too much on technical skill, and a candidate's personality is overlooked.

In almost every core DBA job function mentioned above, the DBA's work is made up of interacting with vendors, users, developers, and managers. With that in mind, the following professional personality traits are, or ought to be, embodied by the successful DBA.

These traits are important for people in almost any profession, but they are particularly important for DBAs. Let it be said of the successful DBA that he or she is self-confident, curious, tenacious, polite, motivated, and a stickler for details.

Self-confidence

DBAs that lack self-confidence, ask the manager's opinion on every decision no matter how large or small, and show no initiative, are not all-star material. This indecision may be acceptable for a new DBA working under the supervision of a senior DBA, but the DBA must learn to depend on his or her own judgment for important decisions.

In interviews, questions must be asked about problems encountered and how the applicant would resolve the problems. Answers provided should reflect self-confidence.

A Curious Nature

Curiosity is a core trait of the DBA because the Oracle database system is constantly changing, and those changes are not always documented. A DBA who is not curious is passive and reactive, while a curious DBA is proactive. The proactive DBA will install the latest version of Oracle and find enhancements that will make it easier to monitor and tune performance.

The curious DBA invests personal money to stay current. In interviews with potential DBAs, questions should be asked about the books and subscriptions the candidate relies upon. Needless to say, answers indicating sole reliance on "the documentation set" are not an indication of professional curiosity.

Because curiosity is a requirement for a good DBA, another set of interview questions should involve the Oracle data dictionary and the constant flow of new utilities and packages provided by Oracle. A top-flight DBA is not lacking in awareness of the data dictionary tables and views and of the basic utilities and packages provided by Oracle.

A Tenacious Disposition

Like most disciplines in the IT industry, bulldog-like tenacity is required for troubleshooting as a DBA. The DBA should enjoy knuckling down on a problem and not giving up until an answer is found.

In the Oracle forums, thousands of questions have been posted by DBAs out in the field. Many times, the questions are about things that would have been solved if the DBA had been tenacious and curious instead of giving up.

Polite Manners

A DBA works closely with other people. Therefore, tact is required when dealing with developers, managers, and users.

But, here's a fact of DBA life. Project managers, developers, and users will bring unreasonable requests and impossible deadlines forth. Interpersonal skills must be cultivated by the DBA to respond to such requests without burning bridges. Ill-will is fostered outside the Oracle department by a rude DBA. The DBA must be extra polite, beginning in the job interview.

Self-Motivating

Employers value self-starting employees who require little supervision. Twice as much self-motivation is expected from the Oracle DBA than other IT professionals, primarily because the Oracle DBA must often take charge of critical database related projects. In addition, successful DBAs prevent fires before they start, and smart DBAs know what things can cause trouble if they are ignored.

A self-motivated DBA will have a history of writing scripts to monitor SGA usage items, such as table sizes and tablespace usage, and will have significant experience in automating their daily activities.

In an interview, the successful DBA is able to respond to questions about PL/SQL, SQL, and SQL*Plus by talking about the many scripts he or she has developed. Note that many operations in PL/SQL and SQL*Plus are used exclusively by DBAs. Therefore, the interviewer can craft questions about specific techniques to identify candidates who have actually written their own scripts.

Detail Orientation

Being detail-oriented is perhaps the most important trait for a DBA. Oracle DBAs are often described as having an "anal" personality, after Sigmund Freud's theory of anal-retentive personalities. A good Oracle professional should not have to be told to crosscheck details or to document quirks observed during an installation. A detail-oriented person is early for an appointment and brings a PDA or calendar to an interview. Questions asked by the detail-oriented person are reflections of the research conducted about the potential new employer.

Conclusion

This chapter has been concerned with the specific criteria for evaluating work and academic history. Next, let's look at the roles of Oracle professionals and get more insights into the characteristics of a successful Oracle professional.

Chapter 3

Roles for the Oracle Professional

A good Oracle candidate is able to articulate a solid knowledge of techniques in all areas of Oracle, including installation, configuration management, system security, monitoring and tuning, backup and recovery strategies, and troubleshooting. In addition, a successful Oracle professional in any organization must also possess above average communication skills.

Oracle DBA Job Roles

The job of Oracle Database Administrator means many things to many people. What the new DBA does is determined by the size of the employer. In a small shop, the DBA's duties are much broader than in corporations with teams of DBAs dedicated to specific projects.

Is the employer doing development? Is it utilizing a third party package? The functions of the DBA position are also determined by the answers to those questions. The interviewee and the interviewer must be prepared to discuss and understand what is expected of the DBA and the role of the DBA within the company hierarchy.

When developers design an application, the DBA's duties include creating primary database objects, such as database storage structures (tablespaces), tables, indexes, and views. The database structure is modified by the DBA on an as-needed basis, based on information provided by developers. Perhaps the most important of the DBA's duties is to monitor and optimize the performance of the database. Here are some common job duties for the Oracle database professional:

- **User Management** - The DBA is responsible for enrolling users and maintaining system security.

- **Storage Management** - Allocation of system storage and plans for future storage requirements for the database are duties of the DBA. Archived data must be maintained on appropriate storage devices.

- **Disaster Recovery** - A key duty of the DBA is to back up and restore the database or communicate backup requirements to the storage management team.

- **Hardware Management** - Installation and upgrades to the ORACLE Server and application tools are often performed by the DBA.

- **Oracle and End-user Liaison** - In contacting Oracle Corporation for technical support, the Oracle DBA becomes the official company representative and contact point with Oracle Corporation. Compliance with Oracle License agreements is also insured by the DBA.

To sum up, a full-charge Oracle DBA candidate is knowledgeable in installation, configuration management, system security, monitoring and tuning techniques, backup and recovery strategies, vendor relations, and of course, the day-to-day honor of chief troubleshooter.

Let's drill-down and review the basic knowledge areas for the Oracle DBA candidate.

Installation

Because each platform is different, the successful DBA stays current regarding installation and updates on the platform against which a system is running. Staying current isn't easy. A DBA accustomed to working under Windows NT may have trouble with a UNIX or DEC-VAX installation. Incorrect updates performed on production machines can result in big trouble.

In interviews for a DBA position, questions about installing and upgrading Oracle systems are to be expected. The candidate should be prepared to discuss his or her platform and any modifications to the standard installation that exist upon it.

Configuration Management

A successful DBA is able to manage configuration, including sizing the database, placing files, and specifying storage media. The DBA is also informed about RAID levels, disk sharing, disk shadowing, solid-state disks, optical storage, and the application of those methods in the Oracle environment. With regard to UNIX, a DBA's understanding is expected to include the cost and benefits associated with use of raw devices and the circumstances under which raw device usage becomes mandatory.

System Security

Having a clear understanding of Oracle security options is fundamental to the DBA skill set. Specifically, knowledge of system and object level privileges, roles, and profiles must be demonstrated. Knowledge of how to integrate operating system security options with the Oracle options is vital. In some shops, knowing how to use Secure Oracle and implement Oracle*Net is a job requirement.

Monitoring and Tuning

Part of the DBA's daily routine is monitoring and tuning the database and associated applications. The DBA's knowledge base must include detailed understanding of the Oracle data dictionary, the TKPROF and explain plan utilities, as well as the cost-based and rule-based optimizers. A top-notch DBA is able to maximize the benefits of indexing, use hints, and knows how to tune SQL statements.

In interviewing for a DBA position, candidates should be prepared to discuss DBA_ views, ALL_ views, USER_ views, SYS owned "$" tables, and V$ dynamic performance tables, which are part of the Oracle data dictionary.

Interviewers are also interested in candidates who are familiar with the DBMS_* series of packages and how to use them for tuning and script development. When the discussion turns to tuning and monitoring, the candidate should be able to discuss usage of the UTL*.SQL series of utility scripts.

Backup and Recovery Strategies

A DBA candidate's understanding of Oracle's backup and recovery options may be discovered by questions covering the import and export utilities, use of cold and hot backups, and recovery scenarios involving partial recovery at the table, tablespace, and database levels.

Troubleshooting

The flair for troubleshooting is a characteristic that is not common to all people. The art of troubleshooting requires an analytical approach, where the problem is laid out in discrete parts, and each is attacked in a methodical fashion until the problem can be resolved.

Troubleshooting sometimes requires the DBA to admit he or she does not know something and must have the wherewithal to look for the answer. In responding to questions about troubleshooting, the DBA candidate should be prepared to discuss real-life experiences. The best examples are those illustrating a lot of thought and multiple troubleshooting steps.

Communication Skills

Great technical skills are needed by the DBA, but technical knowledge alone does not guarantee job success. As mentioned earlier, a DBA needs to be polite when dealing with fellow DBAs, managers, vendors, and end users. Because a significant percentage of the DBA's work requires interacting with others on multiple levels, DBAs must be able to speak, think, and write clearly and concisely. A DBA should strive to set the standard for quality oral and written communication skills.

An inventory of a DBA's communication skills starts with the professional résumé. A DBA's résumé should be easy to read and reflect the candidate's publishing and speaking credits. Whether the DBA was a keynote speaker at a national conference or merely presented a topic at a local user group, those experiences document the candidate's communication skills.

The interviewer should bring questions about job experiences that required the candidate to write documentation or procedures. It should be assumed that candidates with an advanced degree, such as a Masters' or PhD, have well-developed writing skills, or they would not have reached that level of education. Candidates are encouraged to bring to the interview their dissertations or other writing samples.

A successful DBA absolutely must possess strong verbal communication skills. The ability to listen is just as important as the ability to speak clearly. The professional DBA's daily routine will include listening to complaints and requests, processing that information, and providing responses and instructions.

Conclusion

In sum, the Oracle professional must have a well-rounded skill set, and not just technical skills. Next, let's explore screen techniques for Oracle professionals and examine techniques and tools for verifying technical skill.

Chapter 4

Initial Screening of the Oracle Professional

While reviewing hundreds of applications for a single job, the IT manager must quickly weed-out "posers" and job candidates who do not know their own limitations. To be efficient, the Oracle manager must quickly drill-down and identify the best three candidates to invite for an in-depth technical interview by an experienced Oracle DBA. Shops that do not have a current Oracle DBA generally hire an Oracle DBA consultant for this task.

Remember, all Oracle professionals are not created equal. They range from the DBBS (Database Baby Sitter) level to a fully skilled, fire-breathing DBA with extensive credentials. What level of Oracle professional does the company require? Consider what happens if a fire-breathing DBA is employed in a position that requires only monitoring and backing up of an older version of Oracle. That fire-breather will soon grow bored and find fertile databases elsewhere. On the other hand, hiring a DBBS for a slot that requires tenacity, drive, initiative, and top-shelf troubleshooting skills is begging for disappointment.

It is not easy to match the right candidate for a given job. Given the choice between someone who could re-write Oracle from scratch (but lacked certain personality skills) and a technically inexperienced Oracle professional who demonstrates the personality traits mentioned above, the less experienced candidate is frequently the best choice.

The typical Database Baby Sitter usually has a good-looking résumé that is full of projects and jobs involving Oracle. However, the interviewer must subtract points if that work involved third-party applications that were pre-installed and the DBA's main duties were monitoring. When the candidate can't answer in-depth questions concerning the DBA_ views or the V$ tables, the person is a DBBS rather than DBA-level candidate.

High scores should be given to candidates who have direct knowledge of Oracle utilities, such as import, export, and the tuning tools TKPROF and explain plan. Extra points should be given to candidates who have knowledge of the DBA task related DBMS_* packages.

A rule of thumb for hiring DBAs is to avoid hiring an overqualified person who won't be happy in a job with minimal responsibilities. In a shop that utilizes a third-party database application that relies on a pre-configured monitoring tool, a DBBS should be hired who can jump into gear whenever the tool identifies a problem.

On the other hand, if a full-charge DBA is needed, a newbie DBBS should not be hired, unless the newbie clearly demonstrates the motivation for high-end learning and the desire to become a full-fledged DBA.

Résumé Evaluation

It is not uncommon to receive hundreds of résumés for a particular Oracle job. The goal of the IT manager (or HR department) is to filter through this mountain of résumés

---

and identify the most-qualified Oracle candidates for the job interview.

Scanning résumés involves two factors: evaluation of work history and academic qualifications. Here are some criteria that have been used by major corporations for résumé screening.

Oracle job candidates used to have only two sources for Oracle knowledge: experience and/or Oracle Corporation training classes. Experience speaks for itself and can be judged as to depth and level of experience. However, any training is only as good as what the candidate puts into the training. In other words, the candidate could either gain much or comparatively little from the experience of Oracle training, depending on whether they took their "will to learn" and curiosity with them to class.

Unfortunately, Oracle University training is not graded, and in the 1990's everyone received "Oracle Masters" certification regardless of his or her participation in the courses. Today, many vendors offer Oracle classes, some of these are vastly superior to Oracle University. Indeed, with the plethora of classes available, it is difficult, if not impossible, to judge the quality of training received by a candidate.

As we have noted, OCP certification (offered by Sylvan Learning Systems) is one benchmark of a modicum of competence. The OCP exam tests the candidate's knowledge in all areas of the professional skill set.

In order to pass, a candidate will in almost all cases need to have had actual experience as an Oracle professional and will need to have knowledge from multiple Oracle references. The test was developed by over a dozen battle-tested, experienced DBAs and has been certified against hundreds of DBA candidates. While obtaining an Oracle certification from this exam is no absolute guarantee that a candidate is fully qualified, it can be used as an acid test to separate the wheat from the chaff.

Developing Questions for Interviews

Interview questions should be diligently researched and the expected answers listed prior to the interview. Where open-ended questions are used, the interviewer should have the level of knowledge required to judge the correctness of the answers given by the candidate.

- The questions should be broken into categories and each should be assigned a point value based on either a scale, such as from 0-5 or according to difficulty. Technically competent personnel should review interview questions for accuracy and applicability.

- At the conclusion of the interview, technical ability evaluation should be based on the results from these points.

- In addition, "open-ended" questions should be included, such as "Describe the most challenging problem you have solved to date", or "Name one item that you have developed that you are most proud of (in Oracle)". These open-ended questions are designed to allow the Oracle job candidate to articulate and demonstrate their communications skills.

As we have repeatedly noted, a candidate's references must always be rigorously checked. Previous employers should be spoken with, if possible, to learn about a candidate's past work history. Many people are good at interviewing but won't necessarily function in the job.

Appropriate Appearance

An Oracle job candidate who doesn't take the time to put the right foot forward by maintaining a proper appearance probably doesn't have the wherewithal to perform adequately in the job. Clean, appropriate clothing and proper grooming show that the candidate is willing to make the effort to please the employer. Candidates who are sloppy in appearance and mannerisms will bring those characteristics to the job and to their interactions with other parts of the company.

Savvy Oracle professionals will adopt the dress of the executive and banking industry. This attire generally includes:

- Crisp white shirt
- Conservative tie
- Dark suit
- Dark leather shoes

Now that we have covered the basics, let's examine techniques for the initial telephone interview.

Telephone Screening Candidates

In the opinion of many Oracle managers, an effective Oracle professional should have plenty of significant real-world experience to supplement technical knowledge. It has become trendy in the past few years to create sub-categories of DBA job roles, such as Development DBA and Production DBA. However, in many large corporations, the DBA is a respected technical guru who participates in all phases of system development, from the initial system analysis to the final physical implementation. Hence, the Oracle DBA generally has significant experience in development, systems analysis, and systems administration.

Unfortunately, many professional job candidates exaggerate or falsify their level of experience. Therefore, the Oracle manager, who may receive a stack of over 100 résumés, must be able to quickly zero-in on the best-qualified candidates to select for an in-depth technical interview.

Generally, the selection of an Oracle professional can be accomplished with the following phases:

1. Initial screening of résumés by HR department (keyword scan)

2. Non-Technical screening by Oracle manager (telephone interview)

3. In-depth technical assessment by a senior Oracle DBA

4. On-site interview (check demeanor, personality, and attitude)

5. Background check (verify employment, education, certification)

6. Written job offer

Oracle DBA consultants are commonly asked to help companies find the best Oracle DBA for a permanent position. Later on, we show some of the questions used when evaluating Oracle DBA candidates for corporate clients.

In today's highly volatile work environment, the average Oracle professional rarely stays with a single employer for a long period of time. While the recession of 2002 created an overabundance of lower-level Oracle professionals, competition remains extremely strong for those Oracle superstars whose skill and background make them indispensable. While some attrition of Oracle professionals is inevitable, there are many techniques that savvy Oracle managers can use to retain their top talent.

Conclusion

In sum, while the recession of 2002 has created a shakeout within the lower ranks of Oracle professionals, Oracle managers remain committed to retaining their top Oracle talent, and those Oracle professionals with specialized skills are still in high demand.

At this point, you should be ready to invite the candidate for an on-site interview. Let's look at an approach to conducting a technical interview to access the candidate's level of technical Oracle knowledge.

Chapter 5

The On-site Technical Interview

During the on-site interview, the Oracle professional needs to be evaluated for technical skills. The following questions were developed in case noone in your organization is qualified to assess the job candidate's skill set. Even without detailed knowledge of Oracle, you can get a vague idea of the technical skills of your Oracle job candidate.

While this quick check can be administered over the telephone, it is often performed on-site by an OCP certified Oracle DBA. Each question is unambiguous with a clear answer.

The interviewer should begin by apologizing for asking pointed technical questions before reading each question verbatim. If a candidate asks for clarification or says that he or she does not understand the question, the interviewer re-reads the question. If the candidate fails to answer a question or answers incorrectly, the interviewer should respond "OK," and move immediately to the next question.

IMPORTANT NOTE:

The intention of this section is not to provide a comprehensive Oracle technical exam, and the technical questions in this code depot are only intended to be examples. The only way to accurately evaluate the Oracle skills of a job applicant is to employ the services of an experienced Oracle DBA and conduct an in-depth technical interview and skills assessment.

Also note that the expected answers from the questions are highly dependent upon the version of Oracle. We have tried to make the questions as version neutral as possible, but each release of Oracle brings hundreds of changes and new features, and these example questions may not be appropriate for your version of Oracle. An experienced Oracle DBA should administer the interview questions presented in this book.

Telephone Pre-interview Questions

If a candidate does not answer all of these simple questions immediately from memory, he or she may not be appropriate for a full-time position as an Oracle DBA and should not be brought-in for an on-site interview.

1. **What SQL statement is used to display the current date?**

   Select sysdate from dual;

2. **You issue an Oracle shutdown command, and after 5 minutes the database does not shut down. What command do you try next?**

   Shutdown immediate;

3. **What SQL command would produce a list of all Oracle data file names?**

Select file_name from dba_data_files;

4. What Oracle parameter is used to define the RAM space to cache data blocks?

db_block_buffers or db_cache_size

5. What is the default password for the SYS user?

change_on_install

6. What does Scott Tiger refer to with Oracle?

Scott is the schema owner for the Oracle EMP demo schema and Tiger is the password.

7. What dictionary view tells the size of each database file?

dba_data_files

8. What web site do you use to log an iTAR? (Pronounced eye-tar)

MetaLink

9. Name the two most common Oracle index structures?

b-tree indexes and bitmap indexes

10. **What system view will display the number of instance-wide disk sorts since startup time?**

v$sysstat

Technical Interview Questions

The following on-site technical assessment questions can help your DBA get an idea about the real Oracle knowledge of the candidate. The following exam questions are presented below. They are especially designed for an oral interview and are scored on a 1-10 scale. The following test sections are presented:

- DBA Sections: SQL/SQL*Plus, PL/SQL, Tuning, Configuration, Trouble shooting

- Developer Sections: SQL/SQL*Plus, PL/SQL, Data Modeling

- Data Modeler: Data Modeling

- All candidates for UNIX shop: UNIX

Tips for Administering the Job Interview Questions

When giving the oral exam, it is important to following these testing procedures:

1. An experienced Oracle DBA should administer these questions. Tell the candidate that you are embarrassed to "have to" give this technical assessment, but that the HR department requires it.

2. Read each question clearly and without elaboration. If the candidate asks for clarification, simply re-read the question verbatim.

3. If the candidate fails to answer a question or asks for clarification, just respond "OK", and move on to the next question.

4. If the candidate indicates that a question does not make sense, or that the question is ambiguous, the interview is normally terminated at that point. These questions are time-tested with hundreds of Oracle job applicants, and they are not unclear or ambiguous.

5. When grading the exams, be sure that you are postured so that you can write notes and scores in private.

PL/SQL Job Interview Questions

1. **Describe the difference between a procedure, function, and anonymous PL/SQL block.**

   Skill Level: Low

   Expected answer: Candidate should mention use of the DECLARE statement. A function must return a value while a procedure doesn't have to.

   Score: _____

   Notes:

   _____

   _____

2. **What is a mutating table error and how can you get around it?**

   Skill Level: Intermediate

   Expected answer: This happens with triggers. It occurs because the trigger is trying to modify a row it is currently using. The usual fix involves either use of views or temporary tables so the database is selecting from one while updating the other.

   Score: _____

Notes:

_____

_____

3. Describe the use of %ROWTYPE and %TYPE in PL/SQL.

Skill Level: Low

Expected answer: %ROWTYPE allows you to associate a variable with an entire table row. The %TYPE associates a variable with a single column type.

Score: _____

Notes:

_____

_____

4. What packages (if any) has Oracle provided for use by developers?

Skill Level: Intermediate to High

Expected answer: Oracle provides the DBMS_ series of packages. There are many which developers should be aware of, such as *dbms_sql, dbms_pipe, dbms_transaction, dbms_lock, dbms_alert, dbms_output, dbms_job, dbms_utility, dbms_ddl, utl_file.* If they can mention a few of these and describe how they used them, even better. If they include the SQL routines provided by Oracle, great, but that is not really what was asked.

Score: _____

Notes:

_____

_____

5. Describe the use of PL/SQL tables.

Skill Level: Intermediate

Expected answer: PL/SQL tables are scalar arrays that can be referenced by a binary integer. They can be used to hold values for use in later queries or calculations. In Oracle 8, they will be able to be of the %ROWTYPE designation, or RECORD.

Score: _____

Notes:

_____

_____

6. When is a declare statement needed?

Skill Level: Low

Expected answer: The DECLARE statement is used in PL/SQL anonymous blocks, such as stand-alone, non-stored PL/SQL procedures. It must come first in a PL/SQL stand-alone file, if it is used.

Score: _____

Notes:

_____

_____

7. **In what order should an open/fetch/loop set of commands in a PL/SQL block be implemented if you use the %NOTFOUND cursor variable in the exit when statement? Why?**

Skill Level: Intermediate

Expected answer: OPEN then FETCH then LOOP followed by the exit when. If not specified in this order, it will result in the final return being done twice because of the way the %NOTFOUND is handled by PL/SQL.

Score: _____

Notes:

_____

_____

8. **What are SQLCODE and SQLERRM and why are they important for PL/SQL developers?**

Skill Level: Intermediate

Expected answer: SQLCODE returns the value of the error number for the last error encountered. The SQLERRM returns the actual error message for the last error encountered. They can be used in exception handling to report, or store in an error log table, the error that occurred in the code. These are especially useful for the WHEN OTHERS exception.

Score: _____

Notes:

_____

_____

9. **How can you find out if a cursor is open within a PL/SQL block?**

Skill Level: Low

Expected answer: Use the %ISOPEN cursor status variable.

Score: _____

Notes:

_____

_____

10. **How can you generate debugging output from PL/SQL?**

Skill Level: Intermediate to High

Expected answer: Use the *dbms_output* package. Another possible method is to just use the SHOW ERROR command, but this only shows errors. The *dbms_output* package can be used to show intermediate results from loops and the status of variables as the procedure is executed. The new package *utl_file* can also be used.

Score: _____

Notes:

_____

_____

11. What are the types of table triggers?

Skill Level: Intermediate to High

Expected Answer: There are 12 types of triggers in PL/SQL that consist of combinations of the BEFORE, AFTER, ROW, TABLE, INSERT, UPDATE, DELETE, and EACH key words. There are also system-level triggers for DDL, server errors, database startup/shutdown, and user login and logoff triggers.

BEFORE ALL ROW INSERT
AFTER ALL ROW INSERT
BEFORE INSERT
AFTER INSERT
Etc.

Score: _____

Notes:

_____

_____

Section average score:

_____

Skill Level: _____

Oracle DBA Job Interview Questions

1. Give one method for transferring a table from one schema to another.

Skill Level: Intermediate

Expected Answer: There are several possible methods, export-import, CREATE TABLE... AS SELECT, or COPY.

Score: _____

Notes:

_____

_____

2. What is the purpose of the IMPORT option IGNORE? What is its default setting?

Skill Level: Low

Expected Answer: The IMPORT IGNORE option tells import to ignore "already exists" errors. If it is not specified, the tables that already exist will be skipped. If it is specified, the error is ignored and the table's data will be inserted. The default value is N.

Score: _____

Notes:

_____

_____

3. **You have a rollback segment in an Oracle8 database that has expanded beyond optimal, how can it be restored to optimal?**

   Skill Level: Low

   Expected answer: Use the alter rollback segment ..... shrink command.

   Score: _____

   Notes:

   _____

   _____

4. **If the DEFAULT and TEMPORARY tablespace clauses are left out of a *create user* command in Oracle8i what happens? Is this bad or good? Why?**

   Skill Level: Low

   Expected answer: The user is assigned the SYSTEM tablespace as a default and temporary tablespace. This is bad because it causes user objects and temporary segments to be placed into the SYSTEM tablespace, resulting in fragmentation and improper table placement (only data dictionary objects and the system rollback segment should be in SYSTEM).

Score: _____

Notes:

_____

_____

5. What are some of the Oracle-provided packages that DBAs should be aware of?

Skill Level: Intermediate to High

Expected answer: Oracle provides a number of packages in the form of the DBMS_ packages owned by the SYS user. The packages used by DBAs may include: *dbms_shared_pool, dbms_utility, dbms_sql, dbms_ddl, dbms_session, dbms_output* and *dbms_snapshot.* They may also try to answer with the UTL*.SQL or CAT*.SQL series of SQL procedures. This can be viewed as extra credit but isn't part of the answer.

Score: _____

Notes:

_____

_____

6. **What happens if the constraint name is left out of a constraint clause?**

Skill Level: Low

Expected answer: The Oracle system will use the default name of SYS_Cxxxx where xxxx is a system-generated number. This is bad since it makes tracking which table the constraint belongs to or what the constraint does harder.

Score: _____

Notes:

_____

_____

7. **What happens if a tablespace clause is left off of a primary key constraint clause?**

Skill Level: Low

Expected answer: This results in the index that is automatically generated being placed in the users default tablespace. Since this will usually be the same tablespace in which the table is being created, this can cause serious performance problems.

Score: _____

Notes:

_____

_____

8. **What is the proper method for disabling and re-enabling a primary key constraint?**

Skill Level: Intermediate

Expected answer: You use the *alter table* command for both. However, for the enable clause you must specify the USING INDEX and TABLESPACE clause for primary keys.

Score: _____

Notes:

_____

_____

9. **What happens if a primary key constraint is disabled and then enabled without fully specifying the index clause?**

Skill Level: Intermediate

Expected answer: The index is created in the user's default tablespace and all sizing information is lost. Oracle does not store this information as a part of the constraint definition but only as part of the index definition. When the constraint is disabled, the index is dropped and the information is gone.

Score: _____

Notes:

_____

_____

10. (On UNIX) When should more than one DB writer process be used? How many should be used?

Skill Level: High

Expected answer: If the UNIX system being used is capable of asynchronous I/O, then only one is required. If the system is not capable of asynchronous I/O, then up to twice the number of disks used by the Oracle number of DB writers should be specified by use of the *db_writers* initialization parameter. Async I/O usually indicates a multi-threaded model for disk access will be used and Oracle states several times that with async I/O most systems don't need multiple db writers. However, in some cases multiple db writers can be helpful. The number varies from twice the number of CPUs to the number of disks that are expected to be used, whichever value is smaller.

Score: _____

Notes:

_____

_____

11. You are using hot backup without being in archivelog mode, can you recover in the event of a failure? Why or why not?

Skill Level: High

Expected answer: You can't use hot backup without being in archivelog mode. So no, you could not recover.

Score: _____

Notes:

_____

_____

12. What causes the "snapshot too old" error? How can this be prevented or mitigated?

Skill Level: Intermediate

Expected answer: This is caused by large or long running transactions that have either wrapped onto their own rollback space or have had another transaction write on part of their rollback space. This can be prevented or mitigated by breaking the transaction into a set of smaller transactions or increasing the size of the rollback segments and their extents.

Score: _____

Notes:

_____

_____

13. How can you tell if a database object is invalid?

Skill Level: Low

Expected answer: By checking the status column of the DBA_, ALL_ or USER_OBJECTS views, depending upon whether you own or only have permission on the view or are using a DBA account.

Score: _____

Notes:

_____

_____

14. A user is getting an ORA-00942 error, yet you know you have granted them permission on the table, what else should you check?

Skill Level: Low

Expected answer: You need to check that the user has specified the full name of the object (select empid from scott.emp; instead of select empid from emp;) or has a synonym that points to the object (create synonym emp for scott.emp;)

Score: _____

Notes:

_____

_____

15. A developer is trying to create a view and the database will not let him. He has the "DEVELOPER" role that has the "CREATE VIEW" system privilege and SELECT grants on the tables he is using, what is the problem?

Skill Level: Intermediate

Expected answer: You need to verify that the developer has direct grants on all tables used in the view. You cannot create a stored object with grants given through views.

Score: _____

Notes:

_____

_____

16. If you have an example table, what is the best way to get sizing data for the production table implementation?

Skill Level: Intermediate

Expected answer: The best way is to analyze the table and then use the data provided in the *dba_tables* view to get the average row length and other pertinent data for the calculation. The quick and dirty way is to look at the number of blocks the table is actually using and ratio the number of rows in the table to its number of blocks against the number of expected rows.

Score: _____

Notes:

_____

_____

17. **How can you find out how many users are currently logged into the database? How can you find their operating system id?**

Skill Level: High

Expected answer: There are several ways. One is to look at the *v$session* or *v$process* views. Another way is to check the *current_logins* parameter in the *v$sysstat* view. Another, if you are on UNIX is to do a *"ps -ef|grep oracle|wc -l"* command, but this only works against a single instance installation.

Score: _____

Notes:

_____

_____

18. A user selects from a sequence and gets back two values, his select is:

SELECT pk_seq.nextval FROM dual;

What is the problem?

Skill Level: Intermediate

Expected answer: Somehow two values have been inserted into the dual table. This table is a single row, single column table that should only have one value in it.

Score: _____

Notes:

_____

_____

19. How can you determine if an index needs to be dropped and rebuilt?

Skill Level: Intermediate

Expected answer: Run the *analyze index* command on the index to validate its structure and then calculate the ratio of LF_ROWS_LEN / $LF\_ROWS\_LEN+DEL\_LF\_ROWS\_LEN$ and if it isn't near 1.0 (i.e. greater than 0.7 or so) then the index should be rebuilt. Or, if the ratio $DEL\_LF\_ROWS\_LEN/$

$LF\_ROWS\_LEN+DEL\_LF\_ROWS\_LEN$ is nearing 0.3.

Score: _____

Notes:

_____

_____

Section average score:

_____

Skill Level: _____

SQL*Plus and SQL Job Interview Questions

1. How can variables be passed to a SQL routine?

Skill Level: Low

Expected answer: By use of the & or double && symbol. For passing in variables, numbers can be used (&1, &2,...,&8) to pass the values after the command into the SQL*Plus session. To be prompted for a specific variable, place the ampersand variable in the code itself:

```
select * from dba_tables where owner=&owner_name;
```

The use of double ampersands tells SQL*Plus to re-substitute the value for each subsequent use of the variable, a single ampersand will cause a re-prompt for the value unless an ACCEPT statement is used to get the value from the user.

Score: _____

Notes:

_____

_____

2. You want to include a carriage return/linefeed in your output from a SQL script, how can you do this?

Skill Level: Intermediate to High

Expected answer: The best method is to use the CHR() function (CHR (10) is a return/linefeed) and the concatenation function "||". Another method, although it is hard to document and is not always portable, is to use the return/linefeed as a part of a quoted string.

Score: _____

Notes:

_____

_____

3. **How can you call a PL/SQL procedure from SQL?**

Skill Level: Intermediate

Expected answer: By use of the EXECUTE (short form EXEC) command. You can also wrap the call in a BEGIN END block and treat it as an anonymous PL/SQL block.

Score: _____

Notes:

_____

_____

4. How do you execute a host operating system command from within SQL?

Skill Level: Low

Expected answer: By use of the exclamation point "!" (In UNIX and some other OS) or the HOST (HO) command.

Score: _____

Notes:

_____

_____

5. You want to use SQL to build SQL, what is this called and give an example.

Skill Level: Intermediate to High

Expected answer: This is called dynamic SQL. An example would be:

```
set lines 90 pages 0 termout off feedback off verify off
spool drop_all.sql
select 'drop user '||username||' cascade;' from dba_users
where username not in ("SYS",'SYSTEM');
spool off
```

Essentially you are looking to see that they know to include a command (in this case DROP USER...CASCADE;) and that you need to concatenate using the '||' the values selected from the database.

Score: _____

Notes:

_____

_____

6. What SQL*Plus command is used to format output from a select?

Skill Level: Low

Expected answer: This is best done with the COLUMN command.

Score: _____

Notes:

_____

_____

7. You want to group the following set of select returns, what can you group on?

```
Max(sum_of_cost), min(sum_of_cost), count(item_no),
item_no
```

Skill Level: Intermediate

Expected answer: The only column that can be grouped on is the "item_no" column, the rest have aggregate functions associated with them.

Score: _____

Notes:

_____

_____

8. What special Oracle feature allows you to specify how the cost based system treats an SQL statement?

Skill Level: Intermediate to High

Expected answer: The COST based system allows the use of *hint*s to control the optimizer path selection. If they can give some example hints such as FIRST ROWS, ALL ROWS, USING INDEX, STAR, even better.

Score: _____

Notes:

_____

_____

9. You want to determine the location of identical rows in a table before attempting to place a unique index on the table, how can this be done?

Skill Level: High

Expected answer: Oracle tables always have one guaranteed unique column, the ROWID column. If you use a min/max function against your ROWID, then select against the proposed primary key you can squeeze out the ROWIDs of the duplicate rows pretty quick. For example:

```
select ROWID from emp e
    where e.ROWID > (select min(x.ROWID)
    from emp x
    where x.emp_no = e.emp_no);
```

In the situation where multiple columns make up the proposed key, they must all be used in the where clause.

Score: _____

Notes:

_____

_____

10. What is a Cartesian product?

Skill Level: Low

Expected answer: A Cartesian product is the result of an unrestricted join of two or more tables. The result set of a three table Cartesian product will have x * y * z number of rows where x, y, z correspond to the number of rows in each table involved in the join. This occurs if there is not at least n-1 joins where n is the number of tables in a SELECT.

Score: _____

Notes:

_____

_____

11. You are joining a local and a remote table, the network manager complains about the traffic involved, how can you reduce the network traffic?

Skill Level: High

Expected answer: Push the processing of the remote data to the remote instance by using a view to pre-select the information for the join. This will result in only the data required for the join being sent across.

Score: _____

Notes:

_____

_____

12. What is the default ordering of an ORDER BY clause in a SELECT statement?

Skill Level: Low

Expected answer: Ascending

Score: _____

Notes:

_____

_____

13. What is TKPROF and how is it used?

Skill Level: Intermediate to High

Expected answer: The TKPROF tool is a tuning tool used to determine CPU and execution times for SQL statements. You use it by first setting *timed_statistics* to true in the initialization file and then turning on tracing for either the entire database via the *sql_trace* parameter or for the session using the *alter session* command. Once the trace file is generated, you run the TKPROF tool against the trace file and then look at the output from the TKPROF tool. This can also be used to generate explain plan output.

Score: _____

Notes:

_____

_____

14. What is *explain plan* and how is it used?

Skill Level: Intermediate to High

Expected answer: The EXPLAIN PLAN command is a tool to tune SQL statements. To use it you must have an *explain_table* generated in the user you are running the explain plan for. This is created using the *utlxplan.sql* script. Once the explain plan table exists, you run the explain plan command giving as its argument the SQL statement to be explained. The *explain_plan* table is then queried to see the execution plan of the statement. Explain plans can also be run using TKPROF.

Score: _____

Notes:

_____

_____

15. How do you set the number of lines on a page of output? The width?

Skill Level: Low

Expected answer: The SET command in SQL*Plus is used to control the number of lines generated per page and the width of those lines, for example, SET PAGESIZE 60 LINESIZE 80 will generate reports that are 60 lines long with a line width of 80 characters. The PAGESIZE and LINESIZE options can be shortened to PAGES and LINES.

Score: _____

Notes:

_____

_____

16. **How do you prevent output from coming to the screen?**

Skill Level: Low

Expected answer: The SET option TERMOUT controls output to the screen. Setting TERMOUT OFF turns off screen output. This option can be shortened to TERM.

Score: _____

Notes:

_____

_____

17. **How do you prevent Oracle from giving you informational messages during and after a SQL statement execution?**

Skill Level: Low

Expected answer: The SET options FEEDBACK and VERIFY can be set to OFF.

Score: _____

Notes:

_____

_____

18. How do you generate file output from SQL?

Skill Level: Low

Expected answer: By use of the SPOOL command

Score: _____

Notes:

_____

_____

Section average score:

_____

Skill Level: _____

Oracle Performance Tuning Job Interview Questions

1. **A tablespace has a table with 300 extents in it. Is this bad? Why or why not?**

   Skill Level: Intermediate

   Expected answer: Multiple extents in and of themselves aren't bad. However, if you also have chained rows, this can hurt performance.

   Score: _____

   Notes:

   _____

   _____

2. **How do you set up tablespaces during an Oracle installation?**

   Skill Level: Low

   Expected answer: You should always attempt to use the Oracle Flexible Architecture standard (or another partitioning scheme) to ensure proper separation of SYSTEM, ROLLBACK, REDO LOG, DATA, TEMPORARY and INDEX segments.

   Score: _____

Notes:

_____

_____

3. **You see multiple fragments in the SYSTEM tablespace, what should you check first?**

Skill Level: Low

Expected answer: Ensure that users don't have the SYSTEM tablespace as their TEMPORARY or DEFAULT tablespace assignment by checking the *dba_users* view.

Score: _____

Notes:

_____

_____

4. **What are some indications that you need to increase or decrease the *shared_pool_size* parameter?**

Skill Level: Intermediate

Expected answer: Poor data dictionary or library cache hit ratios, getting error ORA-04031. Another indication is steadily decreasing performance with all other tuning parameters the same.

Score: _____

Notes:

_____

_____

5. **What is the general guideline for sizing** *db_block_size* **and** *db_file_multiblock_read_count* **for an application that does many full table scans?**

Skill Level: High

Expected answer: Operating Systems almost always read in 64k chunks. The two should have a product equal to 64, a multiple of 64 or the value for read size from your operating system.

Score: _____

Notes:

_____

_____

6. **What is the fastest query method for a table in the RULE based optimizer?**

Skill Level: Intermediate

Expected answer: Fetch by ROWID

Score: _____

Notes:

_____

_____

7. Explain the use of TKPROF? What initialization parameter should be turned on to get full TKPROF output?

Skill Level: High

Expected answer: The TKPROF tool is a tuning tool used to determine CPU and execution times for SQL statements. You use it by first setting *timed_statistics* to true in the initialization file and then turning on tracing for either the entire database via the *sql_trace* parameter or for the session using the alter session command. Once the trace file is generated, you run the TKPROF tool against the trace file, and then look at the output from the TKPROF tool. This can also be used to generate explain plan output.

Score: _____

Notes:

_____

_____

8. When looking at *v$sysstat* you see that sorts (disk) is high. Is this bad or good? If bad, how do you correct it?

Skill Level: Intermediate

Expected answer: If you get excessive disk sorts, this is bad. This indicates you need to tune the sort area parameters in the initialization files. The major sort parameter is the *sort_area_size* parameter.

Score: _____

Notes:

_____

_____

9. **When should you increase copy latches? What parameters control copy latches?**

Skill Level: High

Expected answer: When you get excessive contention for the copy latches as shown by the "redo copy" latch hit ratio, you can increase copy latches via the initialization parameter *log_simultaneous_copies* to twice the number of CPUs on your system.

Score: _____

Notes:

_____

_____

10. **Where can you get a list of all initialization parameters for your instance? How about an indication if they are default settings or have been changed?**

Skill Level: Low

Expected answer: You can look in the *init<sid>.ora* file for an indication of manually set parameters. For all parameters, their value and whether or not the current value is the default value, look in the *v$parameter* view.

Score: _____

Notes:

_____

_____

11. **Describe hit ratio as it pertains to the database buffers. What is the difference between instantaneous and cumulative hit ratio, and which should be used for tuning?**

Skill Level: Intermediate

Expected answer: The hit ratio is a measure of how many times the database was able to read a value from the buffers, versus how many times it had to re-read a data value from the disks. A value greater than 80-90% is good as less could indicate problems. If you simply take the ratio of existing parameters, this will be a cumulative value since the database started. If you do a comparison between pairs of readings based on some arbitrary time span, this is the instantaneous ratio for that time span. Generally speaking, an instantaneous reading gives more valuable data since it will tell you what your instance is doing for the time it was generated over.

Score: _____

Notes:

_____
_____

12. Discuss row chaining, how does it happen? How can you reduce it? How do you correct it?

Skill Level: High

Expected answer: Row chaining occurs when a variable length value is updated, and the length of the new value is longer than the old value and will not fit in the remaining block space. This results in the row chaining to another block. Setting the storage parameters on the table to appropriate values can reduce row chaining. It can be corrected by export and import of the effected table.

Score: _____

Notes:

_____
_____

13. When looking at the estat events report you see that you are getting busy buffer waits. Is this bad? How can you find what is causing it?

Skill Level: High

Expected answer: Buffer busy waits could indicate contention in redo, rollback or data blocks. You need to check the *v$waitstat* view to see what areas are causing the problem. The value of the "count" column tells where the problem is, the "class" column tells you with what. UNDO is rollback segments. DATA is data base buffers.

Score: _____

Notes:

_____

_____

14. **If you see contention for library caches, how can you fix it?**

Skill Level: Intermediate

Expected answer: Increase the size of the shared pool.

Score: _____

Notes:

_____

_____

15. **If you see statistics that deal with "undo", what are they really talking about?**

Skill Level: Intermediate

Expected answer Rollback segments and associated structures.

Score: _____

Notes:

_____

_____

16. If a tablespace has a default *pctincrease* of zero, what will this cause (in relation to the smon process)?

Skill Level: High

Expected answer: The SMON process will not automatically coalesce its free space fragments.

Score: _____

Notes:

_____

_____

17. If a tablespace shows excessive fragmentation, what are some methods to de-fragment the tablespace? (7.1, 7.2 and 7.3 only)

Skill Level: High

Expected answer: In Oracle 7.0 to 7.2, the use of the 'alter session set events immediate trace name coalesce level ts#' command is the easiest way to de-fragment contiguous free space fragmentation. The ts# parameter corresponds to the ts# value found in the ts$ SYS table. In version 7.3, the 'alter tablespace <name> coalesce;' is best. If the free space is not contiguous, then export, drop and import of the tablespace contents may be the only way to reclaim non-contiguous free space.

Score: _____

Notes:

_____

_____

18. **How can you tell if a tablespace has excessive fragmentation?**

Skill Level: Intermediate

Expected Answer: If a select against the *dba_free_space* table shows that the count of a tablespace's extents is greater than the count of its data files, then it is fragmented.

Score: _____

Notes:

_____

_____

19. **You see the following on a status report:**

redo log space requests	23
redo log space wait time	0

Is this something to worry about? What if redo log space wait time is high? How can you fix this?

Skill Level: Intermediate

Expected answer: Since the wait time is zero, no. If the wait time was high, it might indicate a need for more or larger redo logs.

Score: _____

Notes:

_____

_____

20. What can cause a high value for recursive calls? How can this be fixed?

Skill Level: High

Expected answer: A high value for recursive calls is caused by improper cursor usage, excessive dynamic space management actions, and/or excessive statement re-parses. You need to determine the cause and correct it by either re-linking applications to hold cursors, use proper space management techniques (proper storage and sizing) or ensure repeat queries are placed in packages for proper reuse.

Score: _____

Notes:

_____

_____

21. If you see a pin hit ratio of less than 0.8 in the estat library cache report, is this a problem? If so, how do you fix it?

Skill Level: Intermediate

Expected answer: This indicates that the shared pool may be too small. Increase the shared pool size.

Score: _____

Notes:

_____

_____

22. If you see the value for reloads is high in the estat library cache report, is this matter for concern?

Skill Level: Intermediate

Expected answer: Yes, you should strive for zero reloads if possible. If you see excessive reloads, then increase the size of the shared pool.

Score: _____

Notes:

_____

_____

23. You look at the *dba_rollback_segs* view and see that there are a large number of shrinks, and they are of relatively small size, is this a problem? How can it be fixed if it is a problem?

Skill Level: High

Expected answer: A large number of small shrinks indicates a need to increase the size of the rollback segment extents. Ideally you should have no shrinks or a small number of large shrinks. To fix this, just increase the size of the extents and adjust optimal accordingly.

Score: _____

Notes:

_____

_____

24. You look at the *dba_rollback_segs* view and see that you have a large number of wraps, is this a problem?

Skill Level: High

Expected answer: A large number of wraps indicates that your extent size for your rollback segments are probably too small. Increase the size of your extents to reduce the number of wraps. You can look at the average transaction size in the same view to get the information on transaction size.

Score: _____

Notes:

_____

_____

25. **In a system with an average of 40 concurrent users you get the following from a query on rollback extents:**

ROLLBACK	CUR EXTENTS
R01	11
R02	8
R03	12
R04	9
SYSTEM	4

You have room for each to grow by 20 more extents each. Is there a problem? Should you take any action?

Skill Level: Intermediate

Expected answer: No there is not a problem. You have 40 extents showing and an average of 40 concurrent users. Since there is plenty of room to grow, no action is needed.

Score: _____

Notes:

_____
_____

26. You see multiple extents in the temporary tablespace. Is this a problem?

Skill Level: Intermediate

Expected answer: As long as they are all the same size, this isn't a problem. In fact, it can even improve performance, since Oracle will not have to create a new extent when a user needs one.

Score: _____

Notes:

_____
_____

Section average score:

_____

Skill Level: _____

Oracle Installation and Configuration Job Interview Questions

1. Define OFA.

Skill Level: Low

Expected answer: OFA stands for Optimal Flexible Architecture. It is a method of placing directories and files in an Oracle system so that you get the maximum flexibility for future tuning and file placement.

Score: _____

Notes:

_____

_____

2. How do you set up your tablespaces on installation?

Skill Level: Low

Expected answer: The answer here should show an understanding of the separation of redo and rollback, data and indexes, and isolation of SYSTEM tables from other tables. An example would be to specify that at least 7 disk arrays should be used for an Oracle installation so that you can place SYSTEM tablespace on one, redo logs on two (mirrored redo logs), the

TEMPORARY tablespace on another, ROLLBACK tablespace on another, and still have two for DATA and INDEXES. They should indicate how they would handle archive logs and exports, as well. As long as they have a logical plan for combining or further separation, more or less disks can be specified.

Score: _____

Notes:

_____

_____

3. What should be done prior to installing Oracle (for the OS and the disks)?

Skill Level: Low

Expected Answer: Adjust kernel parameters or OS tuning parameters in accordance with installation guide. Be sure enough contiguous disk space is available.

Score: _____

Notes:

_____

_____

4. **You have installed Oracle and you are now setting up the actual instance. You have been waiting an hour for the initialization script to finish, what should you check first to determine if there is a problem?**

Skill Level: Intermediate to High

Expected answer: Check to make sure that the archiver is not stuck. If archive logging is turned on during install, a large number of logs will be created. This can fill up your archive log destination, causing Oracle to stop to wait for more space.

Score: _____

Notes:

_____

_____

5. **When configuring SQLNET on the server what files must be set up?**

Skill Level: Intermediate

Expected answer: INITIALIZATION file, *tnsnames.ora* file, *sqlnet.ora* file, *listener.ora* (unless you are on 8i).

Score: _____

Notes:

_____

_____

6. When configuring SQLNET on the client, what files need to be set up?

Skill Level: Intermediate

Expected answer: sqlnet.ora, tnsnames.ora

Score: _____

Notes:

_____

_____

7. What must be installed with ODBC on the client in order for it to work with Oracle?

Skill Level: Intermediate

Expected answer: SQLNET and PROTOCOL (for example: TCPIP adapter) layers of the transport programs.

Score: _____

Notes:

_____

_____

8. **You have just started a new instance with a large SGA on a busy existing server. Performance is terrible, what should you check for?**

   Skill Level: Intermediate

   Expected answer: The first thing to check with a large SGA is that it is not being swapped out.

   Score: _____

   Notes:

   _____

   _____

9. **What OS user should be used for the first part of an Oracle installation (on UNIX)?**

   Skill Level: Low

   Expected answer: You must use root first.

   Score: _____

   Notes:

   _____

   _____

10. **When should the default values for Oracle initialization parameters be used as is?**

Skill Level: Low

Expected answer: Never

Score: _____

Notes:

_____

_____

11. **How many control files should you have? Where should they be located?**

Skill Level: Low

Expected answer: At least 2 on separate disk spindles. Be sure they say on separate disks, not just file systems.

Score: _____

Notes:

_____

_____

12. **How many redo logs should you have and how should they be configured for maximum recoverability?**

Skill Level: Intermediate

Expected answer: You are required to have at least two. For OFA you should have at least three groups of two redo logs with the two logs each on a separate disk spindle (mirrored by Oracle). The redo logs should not be on raw devices on UNIX, if it can be avoided.

Score: _____

Notes:

_____

_____

13. **You have a simple application with no "hot" tables (i.e. uniform IO and access requirements). How many disk arrays should you have assuming standard layout for SYSTEM, USER, TEMP and ROLLBACK tablespaces?**

Skill Level: Intermediate

Expected answer: At least 7 see disk configuration answer above.

Score: _____

Notes:

_____

_____

Section average score:

_____

Skill Level: _____

Data Modeling Job Interview Questions

1. Describe third normal form?

Skill Level: Low

Expected answer: Something like: In third normal form, all attributes in an entity are related to the primary key and only to the primary key.

Score: _____

Notes:

_____

_____

2. Is the following statement true or false?

"All relational databases must be in third normal form."

Why or why not?

Skill Level: Intermediate

Expected answer: False. While 3NF is good for logical design, most databases, if they have more than just a few tables, will not perform well using full 3NF. Usually, some entities will be denormalized in the logical to physical transfer process.

Score: _____

Notes:

_____

_____

3. What is an ERD?

Skill Level: Low

Expected answer: An ERD is an Entity-Relationship-Diagram. It is used to show the entities and relationships for a database logical model.

Score: _____

Notes:

_____

_____

4. Why are recursive relationships bad? How do you resolve them?

Skill Level: Intermediate

Expected answer: A recursive relationship (one where a table relates to itself) is bad when it is a hard relationship (i.e. neither side is a "may" both are a "must"), as this can result in it not being possible to put in a top or perhaps a bottom of the table. (For example, in the EMPLOYEE table you could not put in the PRESIDENT of the company because he has no boss or the junior janitor because he has no subordinates). These types of relationships are usually resolved by adding a small intersection entity.

Score: _____

Notes:

_____
_____

5. **What does a hard one-to-one relationship mean (one where the relationship on both ends is "must")?**

Skill Level: Low to Intermediate

Expected answer: This means the two entities should probably be made into one entity.

Score: _____

Notes:

_____
_____

6. **How should a many-to-many relationship be handled?**

Skill Level: Intermediate

Expected answer: By adding an intersection entity table

Score: _____

Notes:

_____

_____

7. What is an artificial (derived) primary key? When should an artificial (or derived) primary key be used?

Skill Level: Intermediate

Expected answer: A derived key comes from a sequence. Usually, it is used when a concatenated key becomes too cumbersome to use as a foreign key.

Score: _____

Notes:

_____

_____

8. When should you consider denormalization?

Skill Level: Intermediate

Expected answer: Whenever performance analysis indicates it would be beneficial to do so without compromising data integrity.

Score: _____

Notes:

_____

_____

Section average score:

_____

Skill Level: _____

Oracle UNIX Job Interview Questions

1. How can you determine the space left in a file system?

Skill Level: Low

Expected answer: There are several commands to do this: du, df, or bdf.

Score: _____

Notes:

_____

_____

2. How can you determine the number of SQLNET users logged in to the UNIX system?

Skill Level: Intermediate

Expected answer: SQLNET users will show up with a process unique name that begins with oracle<SID>, if you do a ps -ef|grep oracle<SID>|wc -l , you can get a count of the number of users.

Score: _____

Notes:

_____

_____

3. What command is used to type files to the screen?

Skill Level: Low

Expected answer: cat, more, pg

Score: _____

Notes:

_____

_____

4. What command is used to remove a file?

Skill Level: Low

Expected answer: rm

Score: _____

Notes:

_____

_____

5. Can you remove an open file under UNIX?

Skill Level: Low

Expected answer: Yes

Score: _____

Notes:

_____

_____

6. How do you create a decision tree in a shell script?

Skill Level: Intermediate

Expected answer: Depending on shell, usually a case-esac or an if-endif or fi structure

Score: _____

Notes:

_____

_____

7. What is the purpose of the grep command?

Skill Level: Low

Expected answer: grep is a string search command that parses the specified string from the specified file or files.

Score: _____

Notes:

_____

_____

8. **The system has a program that always includes the word nocomp in its name, how can you determine the number of processes that are using this program?**

Skill Level: Intermediate

Expected answer: ps -ef | grep *nocomp* | wc -l

Score: _____

Notes:

_____

_____

9. **What is an inode?**

Skill Level: Intermediate

Expected answer: An inode is a file status indicator. It is stored in both disk and memory, and tracks file status. There is one inode for each file on the system.

Score: _____

Notes:

_____

_____

10. The system administrator tells you that the system has not been rebooted in 6 months, should he be proud of this?

Skill Level: High

Expected answer: Maybe. Some UNIX systems do not clean up well after themselves. Inode problems and dead user processes can accumulate causing possible performance and corruption problems. Most UNIX systems should have a scheduled periodic reboot so file systems can be checked and cleaned and dead or zombie processes cleared out.

Score: _____

Notes:

_____

_____

11. What is redirection and how is it used?

Skill Level: Intermediate

Expected answer: Redirection is the process by which input or output, to or from a process, is redirected to another process. This can be done using the pipe symbol "|", the greater than symbol ">", or the "tee" command. This is one of the strengths of UNIX which allows the output from one command to be redirected directly into the input of another command.

Score: _____

Notes:

_____

_____

12. How can you find dead processes?

Skill Level: Intermediate

Expected answer: ps -ef|grep zombie -- or -- who -d depending on the system.

Score: _____

Notes:

_____

_____

13. How can you find all the processes on your system?

Skill Level: Low

Expected answer: Use the ps command.

Score: _____

Notes:

_____

_____

14. How can you find your id on a system?

Skill Level: Low

Expected answer: Use the "who am i" command.

Score: _____

Notes:

_____

_____

15. What is the finger command?

Skill Level: Low

Expected answer: The finger command uses data in the passwd file to give information on system users.

Score: _____

Notes:

_____

_____

16. What is the easiest method to create a file on UNIX?

Skill Level: Low

Expected answer: Use the touch command.

Score: _____

Notes:

_____

_____

17. What does >> do?

Skill Level: Intermediate

Expected answer: The ">>" redirection symbol appends the output from the command specified into the file specified. The file must already have been created.

Score: _____

Notes:

_____

_____

18. If you aren't sure what command does a particular UNIX function, what is the best way to determine the command?

Skill Level: Intermediate

Expected answer: The UNIX man -k <value> command will search the main pages for the value specified. Review the results from the command to find the command of interest.

Score: _____

Notes:

_____

_____

Section average score:

_____

Skill Level: _____

Oracle Troubleshooting Job Interview Questions

1. **How can you determine if an Oracle instance is up from the operating system level?**

   Skill Level: Low

   Expected answer: There are several base Oracle processes that will be running on multi-user operating systems. These will be smon, pmon, dbwr and lgwr. Any answer that has them using their operating system process showing feature to check for these is acceptable. For example, on UNIX a ps -ef|grep dbwr will show what instances are up.

   Score: _____

   Notes:

   _____

   _____

2. **Users from the PC clients are getting messages indicating:**

   ```
   ORA-06114: (Cnct err, can't get err txt.  See Servr Msgs &
   Codes Manual)
   ```

   What could the problem be?

   Skill Level: Low

Expected answer: The instance name is probably incorrect in their connection string.

Score: _____

Notes:

_____

_____

3. **Users from the PC clients are getting the following error stack:**

    ```
    ERROR: ORA-01034: ORACLE not available
    ```

    What is the probable cause?

    Skill Level: Low

    Expected answer: The Oracle instance is shutdown that they are trying to access, restart the instance.

    Score: _____

    Notes:

    _____

    _____

4. **How can you determine if the SQLNET process is running for SQLNET V1? How about V2 or NET8?**

    Skill Level: Low

Expected answer. For SQLNET V1, check for the existence of the orasrv process. You can use the command "tcpctl status" to get a full status of the V1 TCPIP server. Other protocols have similar command formats. For SQLNET V2, check for the presence of the LISTENER process(s), or you can issue the command "lsnrctl status".

Score: _____

Notes:

_____

_____

5. **What file will give you Oracle instance status information? Where is it located?**

Skill Level: Low

Expected answer. The alert<SID>.log log. It is located in the directory specified by the *background_dump_dest* parameter in the *v$parameter* table.

Score: _____

Notes:

_____

_____

6. Users aren't being allowed on the system. The following message is received:

```
ORA-00257          archiver is stuck. Connect internal only,
until freed
```

What is the problem?

Skill Level: Intermediate

Expected answer: The archive destination is probably full; backup the archive logs and remove them and the archiver will re-start.

Score: _____

Notes:

_____

_____

7. Where would you look to find out if a redo log was corrupted assuming you are using Oracle mirrored redo logs?

Skill Level: Intermediate

Expected answer: There is no message that comes to the SRVMGR or SQL*Plus programs during startup in this situation. You must check the alert<SID>.log file for this information.

Score: _____

Notes:

_____

_____

8. You attempt to add a datafile and get:

```
ORA-01118:  cannot  add  anymore  datafiles:  limit  of  40
exceeded
```

What is the problem, and how can you fix it?

Skill Level: Intermediate

Expected answer: When the database was created, the db_files parameter in the initialization file was set to 40. You can shutdown and reset this to a higher value, up to the value of *max_datafiles* specified at database creation. If the *max_datafiles* is set to low, you will have to rebuild the control file to increase it before proceeding.

Score: _____

Notes:

_____

_____

9. You look at your fragmentation report and see that smon hasn't coalesced any of your tablespaces, even though you know several have large chunks of contiguous free extents. What is the problem?

Skill Level: High

Expected answer: Check the *dba_tablespaces* view for the value of *pct_increase* for the tablespaces. If *pct_increase* is zero, smon will not coalesce their free space.

Score: _____

Notes:

_____

_____

10. Your users get the following error:

```
ORA-00055    maximum number of DML locks exceeded
```

What is the problem, and how do you fix it?

Skill Level: Intermediate

Expected answer: The number of DML Locks is set by the initialization parameter DML_LOCKS. If this value is set to low, which it is by default, you will get this error. Increase the value of DML_LOCKS. If you are sure that this is just a temporary problem, you can have them wait and then try again later, and the error should clear.

Score: _____

Notes:

_____

_____

11. You get a call from your backup DBA while you are on vacation. He has corrupted all of the control files while playing with the ALTER DATABASE BACKUP CONTROLFILE command. What do you do?

Skill Level: High

Expected answer: As long as all datafiles are safe and he was successful with the BACKUP controlfile command you can do the following:

```
CONNECT INTERNAL
STARTUP MOUNT
(Take any read-only tablespaces offline before next step
ALTER DATABASE DATAFILE .... OFFLINE;)
RECOVER DATABASE USING BACKUP CONTROLFILE
ALTER DATABASE OPEN RESETLOGS;
```

(bring read-only tablespaces back online)

Shutdown and backup the system, then restart.

If they have a recent output file from the ALTER DATABASE BACKUP CONTROL FILE TO TRACE; command, they can use that to recover, as well.

If no backup of the control file is available, then the following will be required:

```
CONNECT INTERNAL
STARTUP NOMOUNT
CREATE CONTROL FILE .....;
```

However, they will need to know all of the datafiles, logfiles, and settings for MAXLOGFILES, MAXLOGMEMBERS, MAXLOGHISTORY, MAXDATAFILES for the database to use the command.

Score: _____

Notes:

_____

_____

Section average score:

_____

Skill Level: _____

Results of the Interview with the Potential Oracle DBA

Interview average score:

_____

Skill Level: _____

Comments:

Index

Burleson Oracle Consulting

Oracle Training – This is a popular option for Oracle shops who want a world-class Oracle instructor at reasonable rates. Burleson-designed courses are consistently top-rated, and we provide on-site Oracle training and Oracle classes at standards that exceed those of other Oracle education providers.

On-site Oracle consulting – Don Burleson is available to travel to your site for short-term Oracle support. Common on-site Oracle consulting support activities include short-term Oracle tuning, Oracle database troubleshooting, Oracle9i migration, Oracle design reviews and Oracle requirements evaluation support. Oracle support and Oracle consulting services are priced by the hour, so you only pay for what you need. These one-time Oracle consulting services commonly include:

- Answering questions from your Oracle DBA technical staff
- Repairing down production Oracle database systems
- One-time Oracle tuning
- Installation of Oracle application packages

Oracle Tuning – Don Burleson wrote the book on Oracle tuning and specializes in improving Oracle performance on Oracle8, Oracle8i and Oracle9i. His best-selling Oracle performance books include *High-Performance Oracle8 Tuning, Oracle High-Performance tuning with STATSPACK*, and *Oracle High-Performance SQL Tuning* by Oracle Press. Don Burleson also specializes in Oracle SQL tuning.

Oracle Monitoring – As the author of the landmark book *Oracle High-Performance Tuning with STATSPACK*, Don Burleson offers a complete Oracle monitoring package, installed and tested on your server.

Oracle Project Management – Don Burleson provides complete Oracle design, starting from the initial concept all the way through implementation. Burleson has a proven history of designing robust and reliable Oracle database architectures and can recommend appropriate hardware, software, tools and Oracle support.

Oracle Data Warehouse Design & Implementation – As the author of *High-Performance Oracle Data Warehousing*, Burleson is often called upon to provide Oracle DBA support for Oracle8 data warehouse projects.

Oracle Design and Oracle Performance Reviews – This is great insurance before your Oracle database goes live. The review ensures that your application will be able to support production user volumes and that it will perform according to your specifications. Burleson is also expert at Oracle scalability, and he can conduct stress testing to ensure that your production database will be able to support high-volume transaction rates.

Oracle New Features Planning – This is a popular service where your specific needs are diagnosed and specific Oracle8i and Oracle9i features are identified for your database. We also provide upgrade services for Oracle applications, including 11i.

Oracle Applications Support - We offer world-class Oracle Applications support and offer the best rates for upgrading Oracle Applications, including 11i.

Remote Oracle DBA Support - BEI Remote DBA offers world-class remote Oracle support for companies that are too small to have a full-time Oracle DBA.

Burleson Oracle Consulting also has a vast network of Oracle consulting contacts and we can supply Oracle professionals for all Oracle projects, from short Oracle engagements to large-scale Oracle projects. BEI only employs consultants with extensive experience and knowledge.

Oracle9i RAC

Oracle Real Application Clusters Configuration and Internals

Mike Ault & Madhu Tumma
ISBN 0-9727513-0-0
Publication Date - June 2003
Retail Price $59.95 / £37.95

Combining the expertise of two world-renowned RAC experts, Oracle9i RAC is the first-of-its-find reference for RAC and TAF technology. Learn from the experts how to quickly optimizer your Oracle clustered server environment for optimal performance and flexibility.

Covering all areas of RAC continuous availability and transparent application failover, this book is indispensable for any Oracle DBA who is charged with configuring and implementing a RAC clusters database.

Mike Ault is one of the world's most famous Oracle authors with 14 books in-print, and Madhu Tumma is a recognized RAC clustering consultant. Together, Ault and Tumma dive deep inside RAC and show you the secrets for quickly implementing and tuning Oracle9i RAC database systems.

http://www.rampant.cc/

Oracle In-Focus

Oracle Utilities

Using Hidden Programs,
Import/Export, SQL*Loader,
Oradebug, Dbverify, Tkprof and More

Includes Oracle 9i

Dave Moore

RAMPANT

Don Burleson
Series Editor

Oracle Utilities

*Using Hidden Programs,
Import/Export, SQL*Loader,
oradebug, Dbverify, Tkprof
and More*

Dave Moore
ISBN 0-9727513-5-1
Publication Date - June 2003
Retail Price $27.95 / £17.95

Written by one of the world's top DBAs and architect of the famous DBXray(tm) product by BMC Software, Dave Moore targets his substantial knowledge of Oracle internals at the Oracle supplied utilities. Intended for Senior Oracle professionals, these powerful utilities are hidden deep inside Oracle and Dave Moore can show you how to unleash the hidden power of these Oracle utilities.

Deep inside the operating system executables there are many utilities are at the fingertips of Oracle professionals, but until now, there has been no advice on how to use these utilities. From tnsping.exe to dbv.exe to wrap.exe, Dave Moore describes each utility and has working examples in the online code depot. Your timesaving from a single script is worth the price of this great book.

http://www.rampant.cc/